Lady of *the* Lake

Published by Lynne Fraser-Andrews
Published September 2021

ISBN: 978-1-3999-0560-2

Book cover and interior design by Paul Stanier, Zaccmedia.com

INTRODUCTION

This is a story about a beautiful, elegant Pointer named Tara and her dog walker, Lynne.

Tara was so elegant that everyone would say, 'she's such a lady.'

Tara lived in the town of Windermere and trotted about Brantfell, Troutbeck, Brockhole, and the surrounding areas near Windermere in Cumbria.

...

Shortly after, I met a man I lived with who said it would be like a marriage without a ring.

I then went to teach in a school in Lancaster, and there, in the school foyer, was a little advert saying, *'What is the meaning of life?' The Alpha Course, St Thomas's Church.*

I went on this course, and it changed my life.

This is it, I thought, *the missing link. This is what I've been looking for all my life.*

What brought me to the Lakes?

In short, I was married. I had everything yet nothing: a beautiful home, a good job, plenty of money, wardrobes full of clothes, holidays abroad, but I fell out of love with my husband as it was a very superficial relationship. So, I got divorced.

It became obvious that I had to leave this man I was living with and go where the Lord wanted to take me. He took me to Bowness in Windermere. I left behind many of my possessions, but this was where Jesus wanted me to be, and through my walking the dog, He began an amazing journey of trust, hope, fun, and restoration.

THE START OF SOMETHING NEW

One day I prayed, 'Oh Lord, I need a job walking a dog for an old man.' I thought of writing some cards offering dog walking and pushing them through some letter boxes of properties near where I lived, but God did it before me!

On Tuesday mornings at my church, I do prayer ministry with a small team of believers, and we serve tea and coffee in the foyer and pray for people in the privacy of the sanctuary.

One of my friends, Julia, was with me, and she knew I had prayed that prayer. At the end of the morning, when we said our goodbyes to our visitors and started to clear up, Julia and I went down the stairs to the basement kitchen to wash up.

The church was built in a quarry, and outside, two young church members, Keish and Ben, were busy painting a mural on a rock face in the courtyard.

We went outside to see what they were doing, and as we walked up to them, Keish said to me, 'Do you want a job walking a dog for an old man?'

'Yes,' I said immediately. I didn't even ask how much I would get paid. I almost couldn't believe it as I had only prayed the prayer three days previously. Julia's mouth dropped open. She could hardly believe my prayer was answered so quickly.

It turned out that Ben and Keish had been walking this beautiful German Pointer for Mr and Mrs Baty, and they needed to give up the job as they were going to Spain to take up new teaching posts. They

THE FIRST AUTUMN

asked me if I would be willing to take the job of walking Tara from the beginning of August and arranged that I would call round and meet Bill Baty, who was now widowed. It was agreed that I would have a few trial runs at walking Tara the Pointer with Keish.

Keish, Tara, and I went for walks around Matson Ground.

She could jump over a drystone wall, and Tara knew all the watering holes. Keish showed me lots of walks. I wondered if I would get lost when left to my own devices.

Each afternoon I would arrive at Bill's bungalow and enter the side door of the garage. Bill would come to his back kitchen door and let Tara into the garage. She would be so excited she would bound around the garage as she couldn't wait to get outdoors. As soon as I had opened the side door to the garden, she would race down the garden path to the back gate, which led to a track. This beautiful area of Windermere leads on to Brantfell, and this place was Tara's vast playground.

What a marvellous blessing to be paid to walk a graceful pet dog in a glorious and stunning location.

It was on these walks that I had some amazing encounters.

I like to call them 'God incidences' and I also had a lot of fun.

I loved my new job. I was so happy walking through Matson Ground on a beautiful, blue-sky, sunny autumn morning, and Tara was racing ahead. I remember looking at the stunning colours of the autumn and kicking up the fallen oak leaves, enjoying the crunch of them under my long green wellies.

I remember thinking, *God is good.*

Thank you, Lord, for putting me in this beautiful place.

I asked the Lord to give me opportunities to speak to people.

COCKSHOTT POINT, PIZZA BEACH

Tara had all sorts of allergies, for which she had monthly injections at the vet's. She was not supposed to have 'junk' food or wheat in her diet. However, Tara liked nothing better than rooting out stale crusts and any other take-away food thrown in the grass around park benches.

We frequently went to Cockshott Point on Lake Windermere, and once we walked through the entrance gate, Tara usually turned right and ran down to a small beach area.

One morning she was very pleased to find some pizza in a box on this beach, and by the time I got to her, she had scoffed the lot.

After this delicious find, every time we went on this walk, she would race down to the same beach, hoping to find an edible treat. Unfortunately, she would sometimes find the remains of barbeques, chicken drum sticks, and lamb-chop bones. I had to swiftly remove them from her mouth!

We frequently went to Cockshott Point on Lake Windermere

HE DIRECTS OUR STEPS

One day I was walking on Brantfell, and I met a family of Americans, and we got talking. It turned out that they were Christians and taking their children on a world tour.

I told them about my church and the Lakes Gospel Choir, and they decided to come and hear the choir that very evening.

I was an alto in the choir, and as we were singing, I saw the American family take their seats in the church hall. I gave them a sneaky wave as our Texan choir director, Robyn, was quite strict, and she preferred us to focus on her directions and not the audience.

The Americans were thrilled to hear us sing from our Brooklyn Tabernacle repertoire (look them up on YouTube).

At the end of the evening, they were introduced to Robyn, and she was delighted to meet some fellow Americans and promptly invited them to lunch.

The next day the family came to our church coffee morning, and they were profoundly blessed by a very moving prayer time.

Before they left, they saw on our notice board an orphanage in India that we were supporting, and they said they would connect with them on their world tour.

All these things happened to this family because I met them whilst walking with Tara. Amazing!

 The Lord directs the steps of the godly.
He delights in every detail of their lives.

(Psalm 37:23)

A NEW ROLE

Sadly, Bill became ill and was in the hospital for two months. As it was an emergency, Tara came to live with me as I couldn't bear her going into kennels.

When Bill returned home, he felt he could no longer look after Tara as he walked with the aid of two sticks and was worried she might inadvertently knock him over.

He asked me to look after Tara in my own home on a permanent basis, for which he would pay me and pay for Tara's food, vet expenses, and boarding fees. I had never intended to have a big dog in my tiny townhouse, but I adored Tara, and she became my most loved pet, a gift from God and my evangelistic companion.

"A Gift from God

Be still, and know
that I am God!

(Psalm 46:10)

TRUST

When Tara came to live with me, I put her bean-bag bed by the radiator in my kitchen. That bed was her special place, her security. I had known Tara for a year when she came to live at my house, and I just couldn't get her to come and sit in the lounge with me. However much I tried to beckon and coax her, she just wouldn't settle in the lounge, and she kept returning to her bean-bag bed in the kitchen.

I said to the Lord, 'Wouldn't you think she'd trust me by now?' and the Lord said, 'Yes, wouldn't you?'

And I thought, *Oh, oh, I know what He's getting at!*

How hard do we find it to trust God?

'I get the message Lord, please help me trust you.'

I solved the problem of getting Tara to sit in the lounge with me and keep me company by making her another bean-bag bed. So, she had two beds: one in the kitchen and one in the lounge.

 Trust in the LORD with all your heart and lean not on your own understanding.

(Proverbs 3:5, NIV)

HAPPY WALK

One Easter, the church family went for a walk around Staveley. It was a lovely spring day, and about thirty folks had turned up. I took Tara, and we all met at Wilf's Café. It was a circular walk, but unfortunately, not a dog-friendly one as it had many stiles.

My pastor warned me that one of the children was frightened of dogs, and I said, 'Don't worry, she won't be by the end of this walk.'

And as it happened, the girl he'd told me about came and asked me if she could hold Tara's lead. She led Tara for the whole walk, about two hours. We came to various stiles, and many of them were high ladder stiles, and as Tara was getting to be a bit of an old girl and less agile, I needed lots of help to get her over each stile. It caused a lot of hilarity and teamwork.

Tara was such a gentle creature, and she allowed us to heave her over each man-made obstacle. The young lady who had been frightened of dogs was very happy looking after Tara. She had enjoyed stroking Tara's silky coat, especially her floppy ears.

'See?' I said to my pastor. 'Tara is so lovable because her nature is to be gentle and quiet.'

A VISIT TO THE VET

T ara loved affection, don't we all? Sometimes, I used to give her a big hug, and she would look at me very strangely. However, generally, she was miss regal princess, very content with her comfortable home and cosy bed.

But she did not like going to the vet's, and as she got older, her fear seemed to only get worse.

On one occasion, she was taken to have her claws clipped, and she howled and screamed, and that was before they touched her. Tara became my devoted companion. Whilst sitting in the waiting room, she would wind herself around my legs or try to sit behind me to hide from the vet. Sometimes, she would have super-strength and drag me to the exit door in an attempt to escape. 'Don't be afraid,' I would say. Tara would lean on me for comfort and reassurance, and I would stroke her tenderly.

Thank you, Lord Jesus, for my pet.

" *Don't be afraid*

Windermere Lake

BRANTFELL

One evening, I took Tara for a walk up Brant-fell, and it was about seven o'clock in the evening, which was unusually late for me to be out with the dog. We were returning home, and we had just come to the last steep field and were about to descend to the road. The view of the whole field was concealed by a small thicket of trees to our right, and just as we arrived at the end of the trees, we saw three deer just standing about three metres from us. They took one look at Tara and shot off across the field. Tara took one quick look at me as if to say, 'I'm off!' She went off in hot pursuit after the deer and soon disappeared from sight.

I stood there quite shocked and said, 'Oh Lord, what am I going to do? I can't possibly run after her. Please bring her safely back to me.' I stood still and waited.

I felt the Lord say, 'Be still, and know that I am God' (Psalm 46:10).

So, I became quite calm and peaceful, and sure enough, a few minutes later, Tara came back totally puffed but looking very happy, as if to say she'd enjoyed that chase.

" . . . I became calm and peaceful

A PRECIOUS INVITATION

One morning at church, Pastor Mike said to me, 'Has Bill invited Jesus into his life?' *Mmmmmm,* I thought, *no, he hasn't.*

So, the next day, when Bill and I were drinking a coffee at his dining table, and Tara was sat by his side, I decided to talk to him.

Now, before Bill retired, he had a very senior position in an insurance company, and I felt the Lord say, 'Tell him this story.'

'You know, Bill, one day two men were talking, and one said to the other, "Where's your wife?" He replied, "I sent her to church to keep up the insurance policy."

His friend said, "Don't you know God doesn't issue joint ones?"'

At this, Bill began to cry. I said to him, 'Would you like to invite Jesus into your life?' and he said 'Yes.' It was a wonderful and very precious moment, and from that day forward, Bill began to read the bible and pray. When he was well enough, he came to church with me.

For God so loved the world that He gave His only begotten Son, that whoever believes in Him should not perish but have everlasting life.

(John 3:16 NKJV)

TARN HOWS

Each week, weather permitting, we used to have a little outing. One of our favourite places to visit was Tarn Hows, as we could hire a mobility scooter from the National Trust for Bill to ride on.

Bill loved the freedom the buggy gave him, and the first time we went around the lake, Tara stayed fairly close to us. But on subsequent visits, Tara had gained confidence, and she was off, in and around the trees and down to the lake. Tara loved to paddle and drink the lake water. There were one or two places where we could sit in the sunshine and enjoy the views. I always carried a few treats for Tara, and sometimes we took a picnic. Bill loved the opportunity to talk to other walkers. He visibly brightened chatting to other visitors, as he could not leave his home without assistance, so these little excursions meant a great deal to him.

The views at Tarn Hows are particularly stunning. Sometimes, Bill went too fast on the buggy, and I had to keep up with him. He thought this was very funny and I would have to ask him to slow down.

It was on one of these walks that Bill said to me, 'I've decided to give you a sum of money as you are so good helping others all the time.'

I was speechless!

A few days later, he gave me a very generous financial gift, and he told me to enjoy spending it.

There is a prayer, 'Oh, Lord, bless me with enough to live and enough to give.' God gives us a spirit of generosity. I had great pleasure in helping others when I saw a financial need.

Each one should give as he has determined in his heart, not reluctantly or under pressure, for God loves a cheerful giver. (2 Corinthians 9:7 EHV)

Matson Ground

Evening View Over Windermere Lake

View of Langdales from Brockhole Terrace

THE GLEBE, BOWNESS ON WINDERMERE

One evening I was walking Tara down on the Glebe, and I was inside the golf course, a popular place with dog walkers.

Dotted along the top of the hill are several park benches, and Tara was running around the golf course when she suddenly turned and ran up to a young man sitting alone on one of the benches. He was sitting playing a didgeridoo of all things. He was a really good-looking guy, and he told me he had recently started work at the Old England Hotel. I told him I was a local and a member of the Lakes Gospel Choir.

He said to me, 'I was so lonely, and I was just sitting here praying and asking the Lord to send someone to speak to me, and your dog ran up.'

I told him that I went to the local evangelical church and that, if he wanted, I would meet him there, the next day being Sunday. We

had quite a chat, and he told me how he had survived cancer and how he originated from Scotland. His home church congregation had prayed for him to be healed from the cancer. He had a miraculous recovery, and several of his nurses and doctors had become believers in Jesus after seeing his cancer-free x-rays.

After this walk, I went to visit Bill, and I said to him, 'You know your dog's on God's payroll; she runs up to people, and I end up making some amazing connections.'

Some need a kind word, some encouragement, or a prayer.

"'I was so lonely . . . and your dog ran up.'

PRAYER AMIDST TRAGEDY

The LORD is close to the brokenhearted

(Psalm 34:18 NIV)

One day, I heard a very sad story about a local lady whose son had been killed by his friend as a hit-and-run driver. The friend had been sent to prison for manslaughter. This devastating story so affected me that I felt I really wanted to meet this lady, and I said, 'Lord, I need to meet this lady and pray with her,' and then I forgot about it as I didn't know who she was.

However, I liked to walk Tara around Lake Windermere near Cockshott Point, and this was a regular walk, and I often met other dog walkers.

One morning, I met this mature lady with a Lancashire accent walking a lovely brown cavalier along the lakeside. We started to chat, and she began to tell me about losing her son in a tragic accident and how a drunk driver, her son's friend, had gone to prison for causing her son's death.

Inwardly I said, *Lord, this is the lady whom I asked to meet.*

Pam started to tell me how she and her husband had coped with their heart-breaking and tragic loss by doing good works. She told me how she had lost her faith and that today of all days, she felt at an all-time low and almost suicidal. Pam and I talked for about fifteen minutes, and then I held her in my arms and prayed with her. 'Lord, please comfort and strengthen this dear woman.'

I met her on several other occasions after this, and I carried my gospel choir CD in my coat pocket in the hope of giving it to her. Quite soon, I saw her on the Glebe, and I was able to give her the CD. I hoped she would play it in her car and draw some comfort from it, especially the track 'My Life Is in His Hands.'

Pam asked me to pray for her daughter, Sally, and her grandson, James.

Listen to Brooklyn Tabernacle Choir, 'My Life Is in His Hands.'

'He will wipe every tear from their eyes. There will be no more death or mourning or crying or pain, for the old order of things has passed away.'

(Revelation 21:4)

MY WONDERFUL ASSISTANT

In the autumn of 2013, I started looking after an elderly, South African lady who had the beginnings of dementia. Tara became my wonderful assistant. The Lord taught me a great deal about relating to others through this job.

Peggy lived with her daughter Erin in a draughty, old house in Troutbeck. One of my duties was to get Peggy up and dressed in the morning. As she didn't know me very well, I used to go into her ground-floor bedroom and shout – because she was deaf – 'Good morning Peggy' and give her a hug and a kiss on the cheek. Sometimes she would reply in Afrikaans. Peggy really liked this greeting, but as the house was very cold, she didn't always want to get out of bed. She could be very difficult, and one day,

I was inspired to call Tara to help out.

Tara was usually relaxing on the lounge carpet as my employer kindly allowed me to bring the dog to work.

Peggy's face would light up when Tara came into her bedroom.

She used to say to the dog, 'How's my baby?' Peggy would cradle Tara's face and fondle her large silky ears. Then she would say to me, 'Have you got sweeties for our baby?' We both knew that she meant dog biscuits, and I would always have plenty of dog treats in my pocket to pass on to Peggy. She loved feeding Tara and often spoke sweet nothings to Tara in Afrikaans.

Tara was so gentle with Peggy; she adored all the love and attention that Peggy lavished on her.

HAVE A SERVANT HEART

Can you imagine it? You are on a cold flagged floor with your hands in a pair of trainers, praying to the Lord to help you to put them on the feet of an eighty-three-year-old lady.

He will humble you and teach you all things through crying out to Him. He will give you his kindness, his gentleness, his patience, and his perseverance.

We had many times of laughter too. When Peggy couldn't remember a word, she would make one up. She called Tara's ear flaps, flops. One

He has made everything beautiful in its time.
(Ecclesiastes 3:11)

day, Tara was running towards us, and her ears were flapping up and down. It made Peggy laugh, and she said, 'Oh, look at the flop, flops.'

Peggy could never remember Tara's name. She called her Sara, Clara, Mara, and so on. Tara didn't mind as long as she was getting treats. Peggy would sit and stroke Tara's head for hours, particularly her ears, and Tara enjoyed a sneaky share of Peggy's meals.

When we went out in the car, Tara used to sit on the backseat and have her head between us. Sometimes, Tara would travel in the car boot, and Peggy would say, 'Is our baby with us?'

On pleasant days, we had a regular walk from Robin Lane through Troutbeck. Peggy always marvelled at God's creation. She had a child-like quality, and the beauty of every flower and leaf enthralled her, and we frequently stopped and smelt the roses.

Sometimes, we sat outside the café sunning ourselves and talking to passing holidaymakers and walkers.

I was always very smug, God forgive me, when we told people we lived in the Lakes. It was truly God's blessing. Those walks were very precious times, and Tara would amble along on her extension lead.

TARA AND THE HEN

Peggy lived in a complex of beautiful old buildings in a natural dip. The house next door to where I worked belonged to an elderly lady called Urma.

Urma had chickens, and sometimes I was invited to collect the eggs from the old hen house. I really enjoyed this as it was such a novelty for a towny like me to go into the smelly henhouse to peer into the dusty darkness looking for 'treasure.' I used to take the eggs I had collected over to the farmhouse, and sometimes I would be given half a dozen to take home.

FEAR

One terrible day, I arrived at the barn complex, and Tara jumped out of the car, and there before us down the track was a brown hen roaming around. Tara's instinct for the chase was triggered by the sight of the hen, so she set off full speed down the track after 'Henny Penny.' I followed in hot pursuit, hoping Urma was out for the day or still in bed. Just then, Tara reappeared with a bunch of tail feathers sticking out of her mouth. Horror of horrors, I was stunned; I couldn't believe what I was seeing.

I quickly grabbed the dog and continued down the track looking for the remains of the hen. After a few steps, I found the hen in shock, lying on a clump of grass. I put my hand lightly on her quivering body and prayed, 'In Jesus's name, I pray the shock and trauma off you, be healed!' I didn't wait to see what happened. I scampered back to Peggy's with Tara on a lead. I wasn't brave enough to confess to Urma because I thought she might ban Tara from the complex. A few days passed, and nothing was said, so I thought, *That's a relief. We are in the clear.*

THE LIE

The following week, I met Urma out walking, and she said to me, 'One of my hens has lost its tail feathers. Do you know anything about it?'

Without hesitation, I said 'No.' And inside my head, I said, *Forgive me, Lord, for I have sinned.*[*]

I was so concerned that Urma would ban Tara from the complex, and I needed my beautiful pet to do my job looking after Peggy.

Needless to say, when I went to look after Peggy, I made sure Tara was on her extension lead before I got her out of the car.

---

[*] I have recently visited Urma, who is now eighty four years of age, taking her a big bunch of flowers, and I told her the hen story. I apologised for my dishonesty, and she has forgiven me. It was a very special meeting tinged with love and lots of laughter.

HE WILL PROVIDE

In January 2015, it was decided that Peggy would go to live in a residential home, and in a few weeks, my job would cease along with my income. I was at peace about this as Peggy now needed professional care, and her daughter and I were quite exhausted.

On the first Monday of my unemployment, I took Tara for her early morning walk to Cockshott Point. We walked along the path that skirts the lake until I came to a little pebble beach, and I sat down on the gravel and looked across the lake.

Tara was having a lovely wander. She liked looking for rabbits in the hedges and paddling in the shallow waters of the lake.

I was sitting there enjoying the sunshine, and I threw up this prayer, 'Well, Lord, what am I going to do now? From now on, I'm working full time for you, and I'm wondering how you are going to provide for me?'

At this moment, a tall, slim lady of senior years approached me. I don't know how we got into a conversation, but it turned out she was staying at the Damson Dene Hotel, and she had woken an hour early and felt prompted to come and walk by the lake.

Somehow I knew she was a Christian, and I told her I had just been praying to the Lord. I didn't go into too much detail, and I was very puzzled when she asked for my name and address. After an enjoyable chat, we parted company and went our separate ways.

Then I took Tara on the second part of her walk, a trip around the Glebe golf course. On returning to my parked car, I found the same slim lady of senior years dashing up to me. It turned out her car was parked just behind mine.

'I'm so glad I've found you,' she said. 'I've been looking everywhere for you because I want to give you this.' She opened her purse and emptied it of twenty-pound notes. This generous lady gave me one hundred and forty pounds, and I tried to refuse the gift, but she said, 'No, everything I have belongs to the Lord, and he is only using me as a vessel to bless you.'

'Thank you, Lord.'

This dear lady also said to me, 'My children say I need Christian counselling for something that haunts me from my past.' I hoped to do some prayer ministry with this lady at a future date, but sadly, she refused my offer.

Sometimes we struggle to let go of past hurts and wounds even though we are commanded in the bible to forgive others and ourselves.

I went home thrilled and overwhelmed by her generosity. God is good all the time.

This event was a wonderful witness to my young Polish lodger, Emma. She had stopped believing in God, and she was amazed to hear my story. Emma kept saying, 'No way!'

In the same week, I was invited to go to a Christian Conference in London, and my admission ticket was gifted to me. My train fare was paid for, and I was given spending money. I had free accommodation in a townhouse near the Cutty Sark in Greenwich, and my wonderful hosts, Simon and Diana, treated me to my meals. I was so blessed.

This is what the Lord will do. He will provide for you in unexpected and miraculous ways.

ENCOURAGEMENT

I was attending a Christian healing retreat as a prayer counsellor, and we had about twelve people to pray with over two and a half days. We help guests to do business with God. Towards the end of their stay, individuals are encouraged to give a testimony of what God has done. At this particular retreat, the group of guests was very small, and I felt the Lord say to me, 'You are to tell your story about Tara.'

Usually, we sit and listened to other guest stories, but I knew the Lord wanted me to encourage others. The IT guy put a lovely picture of Tara on the large screen, and I went to the front of the room to share my story.

I did not know the impact it would have on my audience until lunch break, and many people came up and thanked me.

And on other occasions, individuals would say things like, 'Oh, you are the lady with the wonderful dog story—it was so encouraging.'

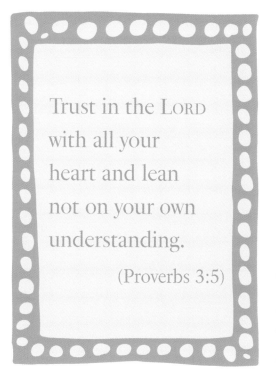

Trust in the LORD with all your heart and lean not on your own understanding.

(Proverbs 3:5)

TARA – NEARING THE END

My beautiful, gentle, graceful Tara was fourteen years old, and she was struggling to walk. The vet explained that it wasn't her legs that were the problem but crushed discs at the base of her spine preventing messages from her brain from getting down to her back legs. Tara was on four lots of medication for other issues, and she was generally fading.

It was becoming increasingly obvious that she couldn't continue much longer. Tara was having very short walks, and her legs were giving way on a daily basis. Her darling eyes were cloudy and questioning, and her appetite was poor.

I had to try to tempt her to eat cooked chicken and fish because she didn't want her biscuits.

At this time, I was volunteering at a Christian Healing Centre when one of the counsellors had a picture in her mind of Jesus walking in a field of abundant fresh green grass. As I took part in the praise and worship time, the Lord Jesus gave me a picture of himself walking in the field, and Tara was walking by his side. Her back legs were fine. I had such a sense of peace as I saw them stroll into the field.

When I prayed, I asked the Lord to help me with Tara, and within moments, I got a message on my mobile phone, and it read, 'Let God take the lead.' I took it to mean Tara's lead.

"Let God take the lead."

THE LADY OF THE LAKE

Dearest Tara was put to sleep in Bill's lounge on Thursday, 24th May, 2018. We both cried. The vet and the veterinary nurse sat quietly whilst Bill said a sweet little prayer thanking Jesus for the gift of the dog and giving her back to him for safekeeping. She was gently wrapped in a soft blanket and carried away.

Bill and I consoled each other.

I went home and took all her belongings to the tip in Ambleside as it would be too painful to keep them. Then I went into Hayes Garden Centre to buy something in memory of Tara.

I walked into the rose section, and I said, 'Lord, will you lead me to a rose that I can plant in memory of Tara?' And within a few steps, there it was—and my favourite colour—a pink, rambling rose, 'the lady of the lake.' *Perfect. The Heavenly Father knows what we need.*

I planted the rose in the border on my patio, and within a few days, out came the most beautiful, delicate, fragrant roses.

" *a pink, rambling rose, 'the lady of the lake.'*

BLUE BIRD

It is very comforting to know that there are scriptures referring to animals in the bible, and I believe that pets are in heaven.

The following week after Tara was put to sleep, a young American lady prayed for me and asked the Lord for a picture for me. She did not know about Tara.

To my amazement, she painted me a picture of a blue bird sitting on a telephone wire, and above it, she wrote:

'All God's creatures got a place in the choir.'

She told me it was a popular song in America, so I said I'd look it up when I got home.

The best version is by Celtic Thunder singers, and I recommend you listen to it as it is a very joyful song.

Some of the lyrics are:

All God's creatures got a place in the choir
some sing low, and some sing higher,
some sing out loud on the telephone wire
some just clap their hands or paws or anything they've got now

GOODBYE BILL

I told Bill about my trip to the garden centre and how Father God had shown me which rose to buy—he was so pleased.

Bill was a very resilient character as he had suffered from poor mobility for many years. Although I was no longer his dog walker, our friendship continued to flourish, and we continued to have a coffee and a chat on a daily basis.

He rang me every evening at six o'clock to wish me goodnight, and I would say, 'God bless you, Bill, sleep well.'

In the month of June, Bill became quite poorly and went into hospital on the 1st of July. Sadly he passed away on the 21st of September.

On my last hospital visit, I was able to sing over him whilst he slept, read him scripture, and pray. Then as soon as I sat down at his bedside, he opened his eyes wide.

Well, I played some music on my phone, and I sang to him again. I held both his hands and prayed over him. The Holy Spirit was with us. Such peace and love were surrounding us.

Goodbye, Bill, look after Tara until we meet again.

The second greatest commandment:

'Love your neighbour as yourself.' (Mark 12:31 NIV)

In my mind, I see Bill fully restored with Tara by his side.

Tara sitting next to Jesus

AND FINALLY ...

When I came to the beautiful Lake District to live, the Lord gave me the following scripture:

But the land you are crossing the Jordan to take possession of is a land of mountains and valleys that drinks rain from heaven.

(Deuteronomy 11:11)

He answered my prayers in amazing and unexpected ways.

He truly blessed me with new friends, the Lakes Gospel Choir, and financial provision through my care work and dog-walking job.

Bill has left me a legacy to continue to work for the Lord wherever He will lead me.

This is part of my story. I have shared it with you to demonstrate that by inviting the Lord Jesus into your life, he will change it for the better.

For I know the plans I have for you,' declares the Lord, 'plans to prosper you and not to harm you, plans to give you hope and a future.

(Jeremiah 29:11)

I honour my dear friends
by writing this story

BILL BATY 1929–2018
and
TARA 2004–2018

EPILOGUE

I f this story has touched you, come to the Lakes and see the glory of God's handiwork.

If you don't know Jesus, then invite him into your life; it will be the best decision you ever make.

When I was a child, I used to sing,

'All things bright and beautiful, all creatures great and small,
All things wise and wonderful, the Lord God made them all.'

And that includes you!